Like our Facebook page
@RiddlesandGiggles

Follow us on Instagram
@RiddlesandGiggles_Official

Questions & Customer Service
hello@riddlesandgiggles.com

Easter Joke Book for Kids

by Riddles and Giggles™

www.riddlesandgiggles.com

FREE BONUS

Get your FREE book download

*Easter Jokes & Would You
Rather for Kids*

- ✓ Contains a collection of Egg-cellent Easter Jokes and Would You Rather Easter-Themed Questions
- ✓ More endless giggles and entertainment for the whole family.

**Claim your FREE book at
www.riddlesandagiggles.com/easter**

Or scan with your phone to
get your free download

TABLE OF CONTENTS

WELCOME

Hi there, Jokester!

Jokes are a great way for people to have fun and share laughs together.

Lots of people love to tell jokes. Some are very funny. Some are just corny. Other jokes make no sense at all. One thing we can agree on about jokes is that kids love them!

I hope you are one of those kids because if you want a collection of funny, corny, and laugh-out-loud jokes, this book is for you!

Easter Jokes for Kids is an awesome collection of good, clean, fun jokes that will make you roll your eyes, snort, giggle, groan, and laugh out loud.

So, grab your Easter sweets and have fun enjoying these Easter jokes.

You can enjoy reading the jokes on your own. You can also share the jokes with everyone around you and take turns reading the jokes out loud.

PSST... you can also color in the Easter pictures and use this book as a coloring book AND a joke book!

TIPS ON HOW TO TELL A JOKE

- Practice reading the joke out loud a few times to help you remember it. You may want to practice reading in front of a mirror.

- Find a family member or friend and ask them if they want to hear a joke.

- As you tell the joke, remember to say it slowly and clearly so people understand every word.

- Adding a small pause helps to build up suspense and can make the joke even funnier.

- Deliver the final punch line. Remember to say it slowly, then wait for the laughs.

- If you mess up, that's ok. Move on and tell another joke. Remember, everyone jokes!

1

EASTER FUN

How will Easter end this year?
With the letter "r."

What do you call an Easter selfie?
A mug shot.

What will this Easter joke do to you?
Make you crack up.

Which books are my favorite?
Books with lots of pictures and hoppy endings.

What does dad do when the traffic light turns green?
He hits the egg-cellerator.

EASTER JOKES FOR KIDS

Which kind of music don't balloons listen to at Easter?

Pop.

What do you call a chicken that is good at math?

A mathma-chicken.

What did one planet say to the other one at Easter?

"Pleased to meteor."

Which month of the year is confused?

A May-be.

Did you hear about the chicken that was alone for Easter?

She had empty nest syndrome.

2

EASTER BUNNY

Why was there smoke coming from
the Easter bunny's car?

Because the egg-zost was broken.

What do you call a bunny with tan lines?

A hot cross bun.

What type of car does an Easter bunny drive?

A yolks wagon.

What did daddy bunny say to his son, who lost the race?

"You only missed it by a hare, son."

Why does an Easter bunny hop?
I don't know—no bunny knows.

Where do bunnies go after getting married?
On a bunny moon.

What happens to bunnies after they get married?
They live hoppily ever after.

What do you call an Easter bunny with fleas?
Bugs Bunny.

What did the Easter bunny do when
he found bugs in his house?
He called the farm-igator.

What do you call a bunny's nose that
is twelve inches long?

A foot.

Which rings do girl bunnies like?

24-carrot gold rings.

What does a ballerina bunny wear in her hair?

A hare net.

What is the Easter bunny's favorite scent?

Per-farm.

Where does the Easter bunny go
if he is not feeling well?

To the farm-acy.

How much ice cream does the Easter bunny eat?
Just two s-coops.

Why are bunnies the luckiest animals ever?
Because they have four rabbit's feet.

Where do bunnies buy books?
The re-tales store.

Why did the Easter bunny go to the doctor?
He was feeling a bit hollow inside.

How long do Easter bunnies party?
Around the cluck.

How can you see if the Easter bunny is hurt?
On an eggs-ray.

Why can't the Easter bunny play golf?
Because he has cotton balls.

What do you say to a chocolate Easter bunny?
"It's been nice gnawing you."

What do you call a chocolate rabbit with an upset tummy?
A runny bunny.

Why does the Easter bunny like skiing?
He likes egg-streme sports.

Which car does an Easter bunny race in?
A hop rod.

EASTER JOKES FOR KIDS

Which sport does the Easter
bunny like to race in?

Formula bun.

What do you get when you cross the
Easter bunny and Winnie the Pooh?

A hunny bunny.

What is a bunny's favorite color?

Ebunny.

How angry does the Mommy Easter Bunny get?

She gets hopping mad.

What did the bunny say about the
thief that stole the Easter eggs?

"How candy do this to us?"

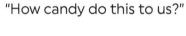

Which Easter specials do bunnies like?
Buy one, get one furry free.

What did the one bunny ask the other one?
"Have you met herbivore?"

What did the bunny say after he got a scare?
"That was a hare-raising experience!"

What did the ear of corn read to the Easter bunny?
His hor-husk-scope.

What does the Easter bunny wear to bed?

Paw-jamas.

What did the Easter bunny say when
all the Easter eggs were gone?

Nothing. He didn't carrot all.

How does the Easter bunny feel about Easter jokes?

He finds them a bit too munch.

Who is the Easter bunny's favorite musician?

Kanye Nest.

How much did the Easter bunny speak at Easter?

Sadly, nest to nothing.

EASTER BUNNY

Why was the chicken disappointed in the Easter bunny?
He was kinder egg-specting more sweets.

Have you heard about the Easter bunny that was a spy?
He was on a steak-out.

EASTER JOKES FOR KIDS

3

ANIMALS

Did you hear about the bear
that ate too many Easter eggs?

He had a s'more tooth.

What did the Easter egg call
the chicken's coop?

Farm-azing!

What do geese shout at Easter?

"All hands on duck!"

How many Easter eggs do geese like?

A duckload.

Why did the chicken put soap in
the baby chicken's mouth?

Because she used fowl language.

What do you call it when chickens cheat at Easter?
Fowl play.

Why don't you see dodos anymore?
Because they are egg-stinct.

Why did the chicken have a car accident at Easter?
Because she fowl asleep at the wheel.

Which type of chickens don't chirp?
The ones made from chocolate.

What do geese call Easter eggs?
A duck-adent meal.

How do chickens play ball?

They wing it.

Which type of dog can tell the time?

A watch-dog.

What do geese like to read at Easter?

Easter Duck-uments.

What do you call a chicken that likes to stay on both sides of the fence?

She is a double cage-ent.

Where do cats go for Easter?

To the purrrade.

EASTER JOKES FOR KIDS

What do you get when you cross a goose with a wolf?
Duck-ota Fanning.

Why does the chicken need to go to school?
Because it needs an egg-ucation.

How early does the duck get up?
At the quack of dawn every morning.

Where does the duckling go when he is sick?
The ducktor.

Which type of movie does the duckling like?
Any duckumentary.

Where do chickens go on dates?
On peck-nics.

Why did the chicken
stop playing cards?
Because it ran out of cluck.

How does a dog like to eat eggs?
Pooched.

How does the rooster wake
up on Easter morning?
With an alarm cluck.

What is a cow's favorite
Easter movie to watch?
Bridget Jones' Dairy.

EASTER JOKES FOR KIDS

What did the duck find between his toes at Easter?

Fun-goose. (eeeeuuuwwww)

Where do fish want to sit at the Easter parade?

In the front roe.

Why do ducks have tail feathers on their bottoms?

So you can't see their butt-quacks.

What do birds give their kids for Easter?

Tweets.

What instrument did the dog play in the Easter parade?

The trom-bone.

Where do cows shop for Easter?
Online cattle-logs.

Who does the Easter chicken have a crush on?
Liam Hens-worth.

Where do horses go for a walk after Easter lunch?
In their neigh-borhood.

What did the cat want for Easter breakfast?
Mice-crispies.

What do you call a chicken that hates math?
A calcu-hater.

Where should dogs not go for Easter?
The flea market.

Which color of Easter eggs is a cat's favorite?
Purrrr-ple.

What did the one piggy say to the other piggy at Easter?
"Don't go bacon my heart."

Why did the puppy have to sit in the corner at Easter?
He bit the hand that fed him.

Why did the tuna complain during the Easter road trip?
Because everyone in the back was
crammed in like sardines.

Who is the most famous chicken of all?
Marco Pollo.

Where do pigs post all of their Easter pictures?
On Instaham!

Did you hear about the cow that is afraid of Easter?
He is a total cow-herd.

How did the dog say goodbye to her friends after Easter?
"Poodle-loo!"

How did the cat know her friend phoned at Easter?
She had collar ID.

Heard about the horse that fell after all the Easter jokes?
He laughed so hard, he couldn't giddyup.

Did you know horses don't like Easter eggs?
They prefer a stable diet.

Which kind of cat steals Easter eggs?
A cheetah.

What car does a cat drive for Easter?
A furrrr-rari.

What do you call an alligator that steals Easter eggs?
A crook-odile.

Where did the sheep go for Easter holiday?
The baaaahamas.

What did the fish say after I told him all my Easter jokes?
He told me to scale back.

The elephant did not like my Easter jokes.
He called them irrelephant.

The seal liked my Easter jokes.
He said they were the sealiest jokes he had ever heard.

Want to know what the tortoise said
about my Easter jokes?
She said that they're turtley not funny!

EASTER JOKES FOR KIDS

Did you hear about the fish that got engaged at Easter?
They decided to make it o-fish-ial.

The fish was in trouble for Easter.
His dad said that he was skating on fin ice.

Heard about the fish that ate all the Easter eggs?
He pleaded gill-ty.

What is the fish's favorite Easter TV show?
Tuna Half Men.

What is the bird's favorite time during Easter?
Cockatiel hour.

ANIMALS

What happened to the bird after Easter?
He was feeling very emu-tional.

What is a baby bird's favorite Easter game to play?
Beak-a-boo.

Where do birds go for a drink during Easter time?
The crow bar.

What is a bird's best subject at school?
Owlgebra.

Who is a bird's favorite musician?
Chick Jagger.

EASTER JOKES FOR KIDS

Who said "Luke, I am
your father"?

Duck Vader.

Who is the chicken's
favorite actress?

Henona Ryder.

Who is the most famous
socialite bird in the world?

Parrot Hilton.

What did the cat say
to her friend who got
no Easter eggs?

She told her to
remain paws-itive.

How does a cat ask
for an Easter egg?

"Paw-lease, may I have
an Easter egg?"

ANIMALS

What did the mommy cat say to the kittens at Easter?

She told them to be paw-lite to the guests
and have good meow-ners at all times.

How does a cat ask to be egg-scused
from the Easter dinner table?

"Paw-don me, please."

Our cat was very lazy at Easter.

She was pro-cat-stinating the whole time.

Which month of the year do monkeys fall from the sky?

During ape-ril showers.

Why are frogs such happy amphibians at Easter?

They just eat whatever bugs them.

EASTER JOKES FOR KIDS

Where do chickens go
to party for Easter?

To hen parties.

Why did the puppy go lie
down after Easter lunch?

Because he was dog tired.

What did the frog say
about the Easter movie?

She thought it was ribbeting.

What did one pig say
to the other pig?

"Stop hogging all the
Easter eggs."

What do you call a bear
with no shoes?

Barefoot.

What did brother chicken say to this sister?

"You really nest up big time today."

What did the mommy cow say to the baby calf
when he couldn't decide on an Easter egg?

"Come on, milk up your mind."

How many Easter eggs did the Mommy hen
hide away for the Easter egg hunt?

One hen-dred.

EASTER EGGS

What did one egg ask the other egg?
"Do you have any good Easter yolks to tell?"

Which day of the week do eggs not like?
Fry-day.

Why can't the Easter eggs watch Netflix?
Their signal is scrambled.

How did you get so many Easter eggs?
I don't know. They just fowl into my lap.

I am so egg-cited about all the chocolate Easter eggs.
I am going to be all oval it!

What is an Easter egg's favorite sport?
Running.

How does an egg look at life?
The sunny-side up.

What did the chicken say to the egg?
"How are you peeling?"

What time does the Easter bunny hand out eggs?
At ten o-cluck.

Have you heard about the twin Easter eggs?
They are as chick as thieves.

What do you call a flexible Easter egg?
A gymnest.

Did you hear about the Easter egg that got electrocuted?
He got a culture choc.

Why do Easter eggs always tell the truth?
Because they believe in being ho-nest.

Where are chocolate Easter eggs born?
In Sweet-zerland.

Where did the chocolate Easter egg
family stay during their vacation?
In a two-sweet bedroom.

EASTER JOKES FOR KIDS

What does a chocolate Easter egg wear when it is feeling cold?

A sugar coat.

Why were the Easter eggs snickering?

They were laughing at an inside yolk.

Did you hear about the beautiful Easter egg?

She had a perfect compl-egg-sion.

What do you call a wise Easter egg?

One that has a lot of eggs-perience.

How does the Easter egg clean her face?

She eggs-foliates.

What do you call a fashion show of Easter eggs?
An eggs-hibition.

How do Easter eggs breathe?
By inhaling and eggs-haling.

What does the Easter egg do when
she wants to wear long hair?
She puts in her egg-stentions.

What do Easter eggs do when they are tired of jokes?
They change the subj-eggt.

Why did the Easter eggs wake up early?
They wanted to see the solar egg-clipse.

What do Easter eggs do when
they are tired?

They take an egg-cation.

Why does the Easter egg save
his pocket money?

Because he is building a nest egg.

Did you hear about the Easter egg
that did so well in school?

He passed with frying colors.

The Easter eggs ran so far away from the kids.

They were all off to a frying start.

What did the Easter egg
do when he got hurt?

He fried out for help.

Who teaches the Easter egg about Easter?
A life poach.

What did the Easter eggs do when they saw the kids?
They scrambled to their feet.

Why was the Easter egg found?
She took the wrong ap-poach.

Why did the Easter egg cry?
Because he can't white his name yet.

Where do the Easter eggs surf the internet?
On the world white web.

What did the chicken say when it saw
all the Easter eggs?
"Chick it out!"

What did the Easter bunny say
about all the Easter eggs?

He said this year there is a nice shell-ection.

Where do Easter eggs go in space?

Into or-beat.

What do you call a decorated Easter egg?

Beat-dazzled.

What did the kid say to the Easter egg
that arrived late for the race?

"Better laid than never."

Where do Easter eggs sleep?

On a bed in the beat-room.

EASTER EGGS

How does the Easter bunny know so
much about Easter eggs?

He has a lot of know-laidge about them.

Why did the Easter egg run away?

He was a-fried of his own shadow.

What type of music do Easter eggs listen to?

Classical music by Beathoven.

What did the Easter egg think of the movie?

It was so beautiful, he fried his eyes out.

What do you call an Easter egg that
has been pushed on its side?

An over easy.

The Easter bunny wanted to know how many Easter jokes I had.

So, I gave him a boil-park figure.

What do you call an Easter egg that is good at gymnastics?

One that has good boil-ance.

What do you call an Easter egg that eats other Easter eggs?

A canni-boil.

What do you call the headmaster of the school for Easter eggs?

A princi-boil.

What do you call the security of an Easter egg village?

The boil-lice.

What game does the Easter bunny and the Easter egg like to play?

Hopscotch.

What did the Easter egg say before the hunt?

"When do we b-egg-in?"

Did you know that Easter eggs can go where they want?

They have complete free range.

EASTER JOKES FOR KIDS

Where did the Easter
egg hide away?

Beat-tween a rock
and a hard place.

Why was the egg in
trouble for Easter?

Because he was in
a no-fry zone.

What did the Easter egg say
to the kid who found it?

"Time fries when you
are having fun."

Whose music do Easter
eggs listen to at Easter?

Egg Sheran.

5

FOOD & EASTER CELEBRATIONS

How does the Easter bunny cook its carrots?
In a hare fryer.

What do you get when you cross
seafood and an Easter rabbit?
The Oyster bunny.

What did the dog say before Easter lunch?
"Bone appetite."

Why did the bread cross the road?
Because he needed to get buttered on both sides.

Why couldn't the chicken go on Easter holiday?
Because he couldn't raise the dough!

What did the Easter
ham say to the bun?

"I will meat you in the middle."

What do bunnies eat
at the movies?

P-hop-corn.

What did grandpa say to
the kids next door?

"It's Easter, we want some
peas and quiet."

What do vegetables
do at Easter?

They celery-brate.

What did the one cabbage
say to the other cabbage?

"Don't kale my vibe!"

Why do herbs belong together?
Because they are mint to be.

How do herbs start an Easter celebration?
They say, "It's party-thyme!"

How do fish do tricks for Easter?
They tell you to pick a cod, any cod!

Where do hamburgers go to dance for Easter?
The meatball.

What did the Easter ham say to the buns?
"Are you bready for this?"

EASTER JOKES FOR KIDS

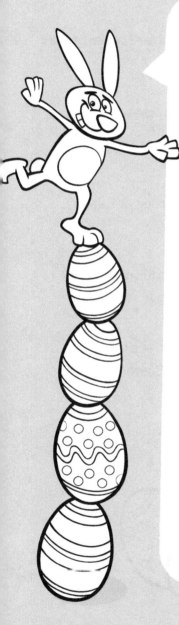

What did the celery say
to the broccoli?

"Stop stalking me."

What did the Easter cookie
say to the oven?

"What am I doughing here?"

Why can't lemons read Easter jokes?

Because they see blurred limes.

What did the lemon say about all
the kids who visited at Easter?

He thought it was a sublime sight.

What did the one fruit
say to the other?

"We make a beautiful Easter pear!"

Why did the banana go to the doctor after Easter break?
He wasn't peeling well.

Heard about the kid that dropped
his hotdog on the floor?
It could've been wurst.

What do you call an orange that parties at Easter?
Out of its rind.

Why did the butcher work overtime during Easter?
He had to make ends meat.

What did the one grape say to the other?
"I feel like raisin the roof for Easter!"

Why did the cheese and the dough fight during Easter?

They both wanted a pizza the action.

The fruit asked to go play outside with this friend.

His mother said it was ok as long as he came back home in one peach.

What did the noodles say to the spice at Easter?

"You make miso hoppy!"

Dad wanted an Italian dessert for Easter lunch.

Mom said we cannoli dream.

What did the donut say to the strawberry at Easter?

"You are a real hidden jam!"

FOOD & EASTER CELEBRATIONS

Did you hear the Easter cake ingredients were fighting?

It was a recipe for disaster.

Did you see the Easter moviewith the dog?

It was a real wiener.

How far does a donut go for Easter?

A hole nine yards.

What is a baby pig's favorite Easter game to play?

Pulled pork.

Did you hear about the fish that got hurt at Easter?

He pulled a mussel.

Why did the grapes have an argument at Easter?
Because one thought the other was being un-raisin-able.

What did the Easter egg say to the peanut at Easter?
"I will Reese you to the top."

How do you measure Easter crackers?
In grahams.

What did the fruit say about my Easter jokes?
He thought they were berry bad.

What happened to the coffee that
did not get any Easter eggs?
He felt a little depresso-ed.

Do you know how the coffee
felt during Easter?

He was frappe-y go lucky!

What did one fruit say
to the other?

"Avo yourself a great
Easter holiday."

Why was the avo tired at Easter?

He did a lot of avocardio.

Did you hear about the bananas who wrestled at Easter?

They had a smash down.

What do you call vegetables that
swim in water for Easter?

Soup-per food.

What did the corn say at Easter?

"You corn rely on me to be there."

Why do buns smell so nice at Easter?

Because they are well bread.

How does bread
dance at Easter?

On its toast.

Why was the cupcake was
sent to jail at Easter?

He was arrested for
baking and entering.

How did the pie say
goodnight at Easter?

"Sleep tart."

Where did the leftover carrot
cake go after Easter?

To the bake scale.

What did the cheese say
to his friend that got left
behind at Easter?

"Cheddar luck next time, pal."

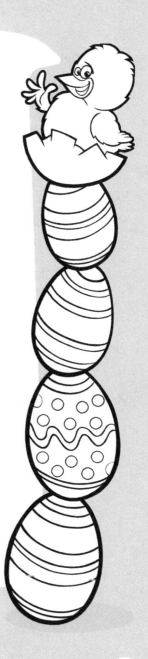

What happened to the lonely cheese at Easter?
He shred a tear because he was alone.

What do you call a strawberry that works out at Easter?
A jam bunny.

What did the cheese do when she saw the Easter bunny?
She ran as fast as her legs curd carry her.

What did one cookie say to the other at Easter?
"Get ready to crumble."

6

SPRING

Why did the trampoline
go to the doctor?

It had a little spring fever.

What is the strongest
animal in the ocean?

A mussel.

Why did the bee
get married?

Because he found
his honey.

Where do trees hide
their valuable items?

In their trunks.

What happened to the frog's
car over Easter break?

It got toad away.

What did the one flower
say to the other flower
that was crying?

"Don't cry. I was just
pollen your leg."

What does the flower
call her BFF?

Bud.

What did the flower
say to her brother?

"Take it or leaf it."

What does a mommy flower
say to a daddy flower?

"I leaf you very much."

What is a flower's favorite band?
Guns 'n Roses.

Where does the daisy go to show off her new dress?
To the flower show.

What is a flower's favorite drink?
Rosé.

What is the tree's favorite song?
Don't Stop Be-leafing.

What does a flower do when it is caught out lying?
It back petals.

What did the flower say when it wanted a kiss?
"Plant one on me."

What is a cactus' favorite song?
Can't Touch This.

What did the sister flower tell her
friend at the flower show?
"You grow, girl!"

What do plants like to do on the weekends?
Netflix and dill.

What do succulents say when they are flirting with girls?

"We're pretty fly for a cacti!"

How did one tree propose to the other?

"Wood you be mine?"

How do trees say goodbye to each other?

"I will seed you later."

What did the singing coach say to the flower?

"Don't sing out of petunia."

What did the baby plant say to his mom?

"I think I've soiled my plants."

What did the wheelbarrow say to the gardener?

"Stop pushing me around!"

EASTER JOKES FOR KIDS

Why is the mountain laughing?
Because this joke is hill-arious!

What do you call two flowers dating?
A budding romance!

What did the daddy flower say to
the baby flower who fell?
"Oopsie daisy!"

Why do kids play all over the playground for Easter?
Because they need to get to the other slide.

Why do bees have sticky hair?
Because they comb their hair with honeycombs.

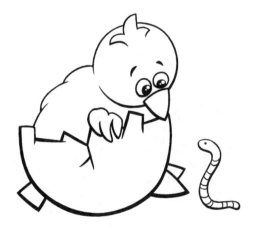

Why did the tree stay at the airport during Easter break?
He was waiting for his trunk.

Where do plants go to school?
The Elm-en-tree school.

How do you make trees laugh?
You tell them a-corny spring joke.

Which month of the year do trees not like?
Sep-timber.

How do trees use the internet?
They simply log on.

How long do trees live?
They come with a lifetime guaran-tree.

How do you make a tree pretty?
You put a ring on it.

How do trees meet friends?
On Timber.

Why does a weeping willow weep?
Because she likes sappy movies.

What does a small plant do when you ask
it a question it does not know?
It shrubs.

What did the tree do when it got
kicked out of kindergarten?

He started his own branch.

Where do trees live?

In Mon-tree-al.

What do you call people that walk past trees?

Pedes-tree-ans.

Where do wild trees go for Easter?

A wilderness re-treet.

What do you call a tree from another planet?

An ex-tree-terrestrial.

EASTER JOKES FOR KIDS

What do you call a group of three trees?
A tree-o.

What do you call a tree with three sides?
A tree-angle.

What do you call three books about trees?
A tree-logy.

Why do trees celebrate spring and Easter?
Because they are tree-ditional.

What do plants wear for spring?
Tree-shirts.

What do you call trees that change color every season?
Tree-formational.

What do you call a tree that skips a day of school?
An absen-tree.

Why do flowers smell nice?
Because they use toile-trees.

What do flowers eat for Easter?
Pas-trees.

What do you get when you cross a chicken and a tree?
A poul-tree.

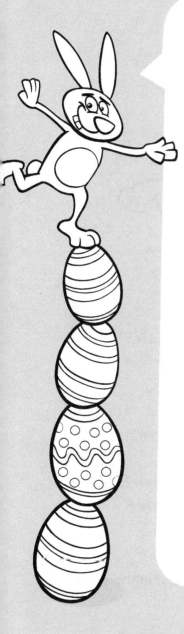

Where do trees store
their groceries?

In a pan-tree.

Where do trees go to have
their teeth fixed?

The dentis-tree.

Where do worms go potty?

In a lava-tree.

Where do you bury dead plants?

In a ceme-tree.

Why was the flower scared
of her shadow?

She thought that something
shady was following her
around the garden.

What do you call a popular plant?
A celebri-tree.

Why couldn't the flower go for a bike ride?
Because the bike lost all its petals.

Why did the gardener plant all his money?
He wanted to make the soil rich.

Why do flowers not move?
Because their feet are firmly planted in the ground.

What is a garden
gnome's favorite drink?

Root beer.

Where do trampolines
go on holiday?

They go on spring break.

Why does mom not
like spring cleaning?

She says it's because
everything bounces
all over the place.

What did one bee
say to the other?

"Swarm today, isn't it?"

BEFORE YOU GO

Did you have fun with those sometimes corny, sometimes punny Easter jokes?

Now that you have gotten the hang of jokes, spend some time thinking up some of your own! Create your own jokes about fun things you like to do.

For Easter, you can create jokes about the Easter Bunny, Easter baskets, Easter traditions, the fun you can have at Easter celebrations, the food you eat for Easter, and the candy you get in your Easter baskets.

Once you think up your own jokes, you can play the game anywhere! It is a great game to play on long road trips, at school, or even when you are waiting in line at the grocery store.

Have fun coming up with your own jokes and endless giggles!

WRITE YOUR OWN JOKES!

Have fun coming up with your own jokes and endless giggles!

WRITE YOUR OWN JOKES!

WRITE YOUR OWN JOKES!

WRITE YOUR OWN JOKES!

WRITE YOUR OWN JOKES!

WRITE YOUR OWN JOKES!

WRITE YOUR OWN JOKES!

WRITE YOUR OWN JOKES!

COLLECT THEM ALL!

Would You
Rather for Kids
Easter Edition

Easter
Joke Book
for Kids

Easter Knock
Knock Joke
Book for Kids

www.riddlesandgiggles.com

REFERENCES

50 funny plant and garden puns that are too clever for their own good. (2019, February 11). It's Me, JD. https://itsmejd.com/plant-garden-puns-that-are-too-clever-for-their-own-good/

Chapman, R. (2020, April 7). 47 easter puns for your egg-cellent sundress snaps on the 'gram. Elite Daily. https://www.elitedaily.com/p/47-easter-puns-for-captions-for-all-of-your-egg-cellent-sundress-snaps-8592951

Food puns. (2018, December 4). Punpedia. https://punpedia.org/food-puns/

Grisafi, P. (2019, October 17). 100+ Easter jokes and puns for all the funny bunnies in your life. Scary Mommy. https://www.scarymommy.com/best-easter-jokes/

Southern Living Editors. (2020, July 27). 40+ funny Easter jokes and puns everyone will love. Southern Living. https://www.southernliving.com/easter/easter-jokes

Tree puns. (2016, September 24). Punpedia. https://punpedia.org/tree-puns/

Made in United States
Troutdale, OR
03/28/2024

18783023R00060